PRINCEWILL LAGANG

Digital Dollars and Global Borders: The Intersection of Technology and Trade

First published by Lagang Princewill 2025

Copyright © 2025 by Princewill Lagang

All rights reserved. No part of this publication may be reproduced, stored or transmitted in any form or by any means, electronic, mechanical, photocopying, recording, scanning, or otherwise without written permission from the publisher. It is illegal to copy this book, post it to a website, or distribute it by any other means without permission.

Princewill Lagang asserts the moral right to be identified as the author of this work.

First edition

This book was professionally typeset on Reedsy.
Find out more at reedsy.com

Contents

1	Introduction	1
2	The Evolution of Global Trade	3
3	Digital Payment Systems and Their Global Reach	5
4	Cryptocurrency and Blockchain Technology	7
5	E-commerce: Breaking Down Barriers	9
6	Technology and Supply Chain Management	11
7	Trade Policies in the Digital Era	13
8	Cybersecurity in Cross-Border Transactions	15
9	Bridging the Digital Divide	17
10	The Role of Artificial Intelligence	19
11	The Future of Digital Currencies	21
12	Ethical Considerations in Digital Trade	23
13	Opportunities and Challenges Ahead	25
14	Conclusion	27

1

Introduction

The digital revolution has fundamentally transformed the way the world engages in trade. In recent years, the rise of online marketplaces, mobile applications, and digital payment systems has created a new landscape for global commerce. As more businesses and consumers embrace e-commerce, traditional boundaries of trade are being redefined. The seamless exchange of goods and services across borders has become not only possible but increasingly efficient, thanks to innovations like blockchain technology and digital currencies. This interconnected world of online transactions is paving the way for a more inclusive, borderless economy that reaches people far and wide.

However, this rapidly evolving digital economy brings its own set of challenges. As businesses go online, they face issues related to cybersecurity, data privacy, and the complex regulatory frameworks that vary from country to country. Moreover, while digital platforms make global trade more accessible, they also present significant hurdles for those without the technological infrastructure or skills to participate. The question of who has access to this digital economy and who is left behind remains a crucial concern. The opportunities may be abundant, but they come with responsibilities and barriers that must be understood and addressed.

This book dives deep into the forces shaping the digital economy, offering insights into both the opportunities it presents and the challenges it creates. It aims to provide readers with a comprehensive understanding of the digital tools and technologies that are reshaping global trade. By exploring topics like e-commerce growth, the potential of blockchain, and the hurdles to digital inclusivity, this work will serve as a guide to navigating the complexities of modern commerce. As the world continues to adapt to this new digital reality, it's essential for businesses, policymakers, and individuals to understand how they can harness the benefits of digital trade while managing its risks.

2

The Evolution of Global Trade

Chapter 1:

The history of global trade begins long before the rise of modern currencies and complex economies. Early human societies engaged in barter systems, exchanging goods and services directly. This system was limited in scope, as it required both parties to have something the other desired. As civilizations grew, so did the need for more structured exchanges. This led to the creation of the first forms of money, such as coins, which made transactions more efficient. Trade routes, like the Silk Road, emerged as key pathways for exchanging goods and ideas across continents. These developments laid the foundation for a global trading system, but it was the emergence of maritime trade and the Age of Exploration in the 15th and 16th centuries that accelerated the expansion of international commerce. The creation of colonial empires and the subsequent establishment of global trade networks connected distant parts of the world.

DIGITAL DOLLARS AND GLOBAL BORDERS: THE INTERSECTION OF TECHNOLOGY AND TRADE

In the modern era, the Industrial Revolution dramatically transformed global trade by introducing mass production and the need for larger, more efficient transportation systems. This era saw the rise of railroads, steamships, and eventually the airplane, all of which allowed for faster and cheaper movement of goods across borders. As nations industrialized, they became increasingly interdependent, relying on each other for raw materials, finished goods, and labor. However, the development of trade was not without challenges. Protectionist policies, tariffs, and trade barriers often hindered free exchange between countries. It wasn't until the 20th century that global trade became more standardized and interconnected, with institutions like the World Trade Organization (WTO) playing a critical role in reducing trade barriers and promoting free trade.

Today, we are witnessing another major transformation in global trade, driven by digital technology. The rise of the internet and advanced communication systems has allowed businesses to operate on a global scale with ease. Digital platforms have enabled the exchange of goods and services across borders without the need for physical proximity. This chapter concludes by noting that the digital transformation of commerce is poised to make trade more accessible and efficient, with technology playing a pivotal role in the future of global exchange.

3

Digital Payment Systems and Their Global Reach

Chapter 2:

Digital payment systems have revolutionized the way transactions are conducted on a global scale. Traditional payment methods, like cash and checks, were limited by geographic and logistical constraints, often creating barriers to international trade. The emergence of digital platforms like PayPal in the early 2000s allowed individuals and businesses to send and receive money across borders with a few clicks, breaking down the barriers that once existed in financial transactions. These systems quickly gained popularity due to their convenience, speed, and ability to handle multiple currencies. As mobile technology advanced, digital wallets and mobile money systems, such as Alipay and M-Pesa, further expanded financial inclusion, especially in regions where access to traditional banking services was limited.

The impact of digital payment systems on global trade cannot be overstated. By providing businesses of all sizes with access to global markets, these systems have democratized the process of conducting international business. Small enterprises in developing countries can now sell goods and services to customers on the other side of the world without needing a physical storefront or relying on complex banking systems. Furthermore, these digital platforms have made cross-border payments faster and more secure, reducing the risk of fraud and delays. As a result, businesses can now conduct transactions with ease, allowing for quicker expansion into new markets.

In addition to benefiting businesses, digital payment systems have also played a crucial role in financial inclusion. In many parts of the world, especially in underdeveloped regions, people previously excluded from the formal banking system now have access to digital payment platforms. This has opened doors to new economic opportunities, such as e-commerce, remittances, and even access to credit. As digital payment systems continue to evolve, they hold the potential to further transform the global financial landscape, making financial services more accessible and fostering greater economic integration across nations.

4

Cryptocurrency and Blockchain Technology

Chapter 3:

Cryptocurrencies, particularly Bitcoin, have emerged as powerful alternatives to traditional forms of money. Powered by blockchain technology, these decentralized digital currencies offer the potential to disrupt the global financial system. Unlike conventional currencies, which are controlled by governments and central banks, cryptocurrencies operate on a peer-to-peer network, making them resistant to inflationary pressures and government interference. This decentralized nature gives them a unique appeal, particularly in countries with unstable economies or authoritarian regimes. Cryptocurrencies have also gained popularity as investment assets, with many viewing them as a hedge against traditional financial systems. Their ability to facilitate borderless transactions without the need for intermediaries has the potential to revolutionize cross-border trade and financial exchanges.

Blockchain technology, the backbone of cryptocurrencies, further enhances their potential by providing a transparent, secure, and tamper-proof record of transactions. This technology has applications beyond digital currencies, including supply chain management, contract execution, and digital identity verification. In the context of global trade, blockchain could streamline processes by eliminating the need for intermediaries, reducing transaction costs, and enhancing transparency. For instance, blockchain-based systems could track the movement of goods across borders, ensuring that every step of the process is verifiable and secure. This would reduce fraud, improve accountability, and enhance trust in international transactions.

Despite its promise, the widespread adoption of cryptocurrencies and blockchain technology faces several challenges. These include regulatory uncertainties, security concerns, and scalability issues. Governments and financial institutions are still grappling with how to regulate and integrate cryptocurrencies into the existing financial system. However, the growing interest in decentralized finance (DeFi) and blockchain-based applications suggests that these technologies will play an increasingly significant role in reshaping the future of global trade. As the technology matures and regulatory frameworks evolve, cryptocurrencies and blockchain have the potential to reduce reliance on centralized financial institutions and create a more efficient, transparent, and inclusive global financial system.

5

E-commerce: Breaking Down Barriers

Chapter 4:

E-commerce has revolutionized the way businesses and consumers interact, breaking down geographical and logistical barriers that once limited trade. In the past, businesses needed physical stores, large inventories, and substantial capital to reach customers beyond their local markets. Today, platforms like Amazon, Alibaba, and Shopify have transformed this dynamic by providing businesses with access to global audiences through online marketplaces. These platforms have made it easier for companies of all sizes to reach customers worldwide, regardless of their location or the size of their operation. E-commerce has leveled the playing field, allowing small businesses to compete with multinational corporations on an equal footing.

The rise of e-commerce has also led to significant changes in consumer behavior. Shopping has become increasingly digital, with consumers now expecting a seamless and personalized experience when buying goods online. The convenience of browsing products, comparing prices, and making purchases from the comfort of one's home has made online shopping the preferred method for many. Moreover, e-commerce platforms have introduced innovative features, such as customer reviews, detailed product information, and easy return policies, which have built trust and credibility in the online shopping experience. This has led to a shift in how businesses approach marketing, customer service, and product distribution, emphasizing the importance of an online presence and digital engagement.

E-commerce has also created new opportunities for businesses in emerging markets. Many companies in developing countries are now able to sell their products to global consumers without the need for physical storefronts or intermediaries. This has opened up access to new revenue streams and allowed businesses to tap into markets they might have previously found difficult to enter. Additionally, the rise of e-commerce has driven the growth of logistics and delivery services, further facilitating global trade. As the sector continues to evolve, innovations in technology, payment systems, and supply chain management will continue to shape the future of e-commerce, ensuring that businesses can reach consumers across the globe more efficiently than ever before.

6

Technology and Supply Chain Management

Chapter 5:

Technology is revolutionizing the way businesses handle their supply chains, offering smarter, more efficient ways to manage logistics and transportation. The integration of the Internet of Things (IoT) has been one of the significant advancements, enabling businesses to track shipments in real time. IoT devices, such as sensors and GPS trackers, provide detailed data about the location, temperature, and condition of goods as they move through the supply chain. This level of monitoring increases transparency, reduces the risk of lost or damaged goods, and ensures that products reach their destinations on time. With the ability to monitor each step in the journey, businesses can respond more quickly to delays or other issues, improving overall operational efficiency.

Artificial Intelligence (AI) is another game-changer in supply chain management. By processing vast amounts of data, AI can identify patterns and predict demand, helping businesses optimize their inventory levels. Predictive analytics powered by AI can forecast demand fluctuations, enabling businesses to adjust their stock levels accordingly and minimize overproduction or stockouts. Additionally, AI-driven algorithms can optimize routes for delivery trucks, reducing fuel consumption and transit time. By applying machine learning techniques, AI can also automate routine tasks, such as order processing and inventory management, freeing up human resources to focus on more strategic activities. These technological innovations are transforming global trade operations, making them faster, more reliable, and cost-effective.

The use of technology in supply chain management extends beyond just tracking and logistics optimization. Blockchain, for example, is being used to create secure and transparent records of transactions throughout the supply chain. Each step in the supply chain can be recorded on a blockchain ledger, providing an immutable and traceable history of the goods from manufacturer to consumer. This improves accountability, reduces fraud, and fosters trust among parties involved in the supply chain. As companies increasingly embrace these tools, the global trade landscape is becoming more interconnected, with technology playing a crucial role in enhancing collaboration, increasing operational efficiency, and ensuring the timely delivery of goods worldwide.

7

Trade Policies in the Digital Era

Chapter 6:

  In today's digital age, the rapid growth of online trade and digital commerce presents new challenges for governments seeking to regulate cross-border transactions. Traditional trade policies, designed for the physical movement of goods, are often ill-suited for the complexities of digital trade, which can span borders in an instant without the need for physical shipping. As a result, governments around the world are grappling with the need to adapt their trade policies to this new era. This includes addressing issues such as data privacy, cross-border data flows, and the regulation of digital services like cloud computing and e-commerce platforms. The evolving nature of digital commerce requires international cooperation and agreement to create trade policies that ensure a fair and competitive global marketplace.

Digital trade policies must also consider the challenges posed by digital taxation. With many companies operating across multiple jurisdictions, determining where and how to tax digital transactions has become increasingly complicated. Governments are working to develop tax frameworks that capture the value created in digital trade without stifling innovation. Additionally, there are concerns about the protection of intellectual property (IP) in the digital realm. The ease of copying and distributing digital goods has led to a rise in piracy and counterfeiting, prompting countries to reevaluate their IP laws and enforcement mechanisms. As governments continue to adjust their trade policies, they must strike a balance between encouraging digital innovation and ensuring that businesses and consumers are protected from unfair practices.

Global trade is increasingly interconnected, and digital policies must consider the implications of these interconnections. Trade agreements in the digital era require greater collaboration between countries to ensure that regulations are harmonized and do not create unnecessary barriers to digital commerce. This is particularly important for developing economies that may lack the infrastructure to fully participate in digital trade. As such, there is a growing need for global institutions, such as the World Trade Organization (WTO), to establish a framework for regulating digital trade that fosters inclusivity, fairness, and growth. By addressing these complexities, governments can create a regulatory environment that supports the growth of digital commerce while safeguarding consumer interests and promoting economic stability.

8

Cybersecurity in Cross-Border Transactions

Chapter 7:

With the rise of digital trade, the threat of cyberattacks has escalated, making cybersecurity a top priority for businesses involved in cross-border transactions. The internet has made it easier for companies to conduct global transactions, but it has also opened the door to cybercriminals looking to exploit vulnerabilities in digital systems. Cybersecurity breaches can have far-reaching consequences, from the loss of sensitive financial data to the disruption of global supply chains. As a result, companies must invest in robust cybersecurity measures to protect their systems and ensure the safety of transactions. This includes encrypting sensitive data, implementing multi-factor authentication, and regularly updating software to address emerging threats.

The complexity of cross-border transactions further complicates the issue of cybersecurity. When data crosses national borders, it may be subject to different privacy laws and regulations, which can create challenges for businesses trying to ensure compliance. Companies operating internationally must navigate a patchwork of cybersecurity laws and regulations, which vary from country to country. This increases the risk of non-compliance and exposes businesses to potential fines or legal action. Moreover, the anonymity provided by the internet makes it difficult for authorities to trace cybercriminals, further complicating efforts to safeguard digital trade. Therefore, international cooperation is essential to establish common cybersecurity standards and protocols that can help protect businesses and consumers from cyber threats.

To enhance cybersecurity in cross-border transactions, businesses must also focus on fostering a culture of security within their organizations. This includes training employees to recognize phishing attempts, safeguarding passwords, and promoting best practices for handling sensitive information. Cybersecurity is not just the responsibility of IT departments but must be ingrained in the company's overall strategy. Collaboration between private companies, governments, and international organizations is key to creating a secure environment for global trade. By sharing threat intelligence and best practices, businesses and governments can work together to combat the growing threat of cybercrime and ensure the continued growth of digital commerce.

9

Bridging the Digital Divide

Chapter 8:

While digital technology is transforming global trade, not all countries or communities have equal access to the digital tools and resources necessary to participate in the global economy. The digital divide, or the gap between those who have access to technology and those who do not, presents a significant barrier to inclusive economic growth. In many developing nations, limited access to the internet, outdated infrastructure, and a lack of digital literacy prevent individuals and businesses from fully participating in digital trade. As a result, these countries miss out on the economic opportunities that digital commerce offers, which can further exacerbate inequalities in wealth and development. Addressing the digital divide is crucial to ensuring that all nations can benefit from the opportunities presented by the digital economy.

Efforts to bridge the digital divide require significant investments in infrastructure, education, and policy development. Governments and international organizations must work together to build the necessary digital infrastructure, such as reliable internet connections, to ensure that people in underserved areas can connect to the global marketplace. This includes extending internet access to rural and remote areas, where connectivity is often limited or nonexistent. Additionally, digital literacy programs are essential to empower individuals and businesses to take advantage of digital trade opportunities. These programs can teach essential skills such as e-commerce, online marketing, and digital payment systems, enabling people to participate in the digital economy and compete on a global scale.

Bridging the digital divide is not only about infrastructure and education but also about creating an enabling policy environment that supports digital inclusion. Governments must ensure that their policies promote equitable access to digital resources, particularly for marginalized groups. This includes addressing issues such as affordability, language barriers, and accessibility for people with disabilities. Additionally, international cooperation is necessary to create a global framework that encourages digital inclusion and ensures that all nations, regardless of their level of development, have the opportunity to participate in global trade. By bridging the digital divide, we can create a more inclusive global economy that offers equal opportunities for all.

10

The Role of Artificial Intelligence

Chapter 9:

Artificial intelligence (AI) has emerged as a transformative force in the world of trade, revolutionizing decision-making processes and enhancing operational efficiency. AI's capacity to analyze vast amounts of data in real-time allows businesses to gain insights into market trends and consumer behavior, making them better equipped to respond to market dynamics. Machine learning algorithms, a key component of AI, enable systems to continuously improve their ability to predict future market shifts, optimizing strategies and reducing risk. In the context of trade, AI has made it possible for companies to act on insights quickly, allowing them to stay ahead of competitors in a fast-paced, ever-evolving global market.

Beyond market analysis, AI is also redefining how businesses engage with their customers. By employing natural language processing (NLP) and chatbots, businesses can provide personalized and timely customer support, ensuring high levels of satisfaction and loyalty. These AI-driven systems can handle customer queries, resolve issues, and even predict future needs based on past interactions. As AI continues to evolve, the customer experience becomes increasingly automated, yet more intuitive, providing customers with faster, more relevant solutions. This shift is especially evident in e-commerce, where AI plays a significant role in tailoring product recommendations and advertising strategies to individual preferences, enhancing both the consumer experience and the effectiveness of marketing campaigns.

In logistics, AI is optimizing supply chain management, transforming how goods are moved globally. Machine learning algorithms predict demand fluctuations, enabling businesses to adjust inventory levels and streamline shipping processes. AI-powered automation is improving warehouse operations, with robots and drones taking on tasks such as sorting, packaging, and delivery. This automation reduces human error, enhances efficiency, and lowers costs, making the entire logistics process more agile. As AI continues to make inroads in trade, it offers the promise of even smarter systems, which could lead to fully autonomous supply chains capable of responding dynamically to changing global conditions.

11

The Future of Digital Currencies

Chapter 10:

The rise of digital currencies is reshaping the landscape of global finance, with central banks around the world exploring their potential to drive economic growth and stability. These digital currencies, often referred to as Central Bank Digital Currencies (CBDCs), are seen as an efficient and secure alternative to traditional fiat currencies. By leveraging blockchain technology, CBDCs offer a decentralized platform that enhances transparency, reduces the risks of fraud, and simplifies cross-border transactions. Unlike cryptocurrencies such as Bitcoin, which can be volatile, CBDCs are typically backed by governments, offering greater stability and regulatory oversight, which may foster trust among users.

One of the most compelling advantages of digital currencies is their ability to facilitate seamless global transactions. With digital currencies, the need for intermediaries like banks and payment processors can be eliminated, making international trade faster and cheaper. Traditional banking systems often rely on slow and expensive cross-border payment networks, but digital currencies can enable near-instant transactions at a fraction of the cost. This can unlock new opportunities for businesses, especially in developing regions, by reducing barriers to entry and promoting greater financial inclusion. As the world becomes more interconnected, digital currencies could play a pivotal role in streamlining global commerce and enhancing economic ties between nations.

However, the widespread adoption of digital currencies also presents challenges, particularly concerning security and privacy. As governments move toward issuing their own digital currencies, questions arise about surveillance and control over individuals' financial transactions. There is also the risk of cyberattacks, which could compromise the integrity of digital currency systems. Additionally, the potential for digital currencies to destabilize existing financial systems and challenge the role of traditional banking is a concern for policymakers. As the future of digital currencies unfolds, governments, financial institutions, and businesses will need to strike a balance between innovation, regulation, and security to ensure that these new forms of currency foster economic growth without compromising financial stability.

12

Ethical Considerations in Digital Trade

Chapter 11:

As technology continues to drive the evolution of global trade, it raises important ethical considerations that must be addressed. One of the primary concerns is data privacy, as digital transactions and e-commerce rely heavily on the collection and use of personal data. The potential for misuse of this data by businesses or governments poses a significant risk to individuals' privacy rights. Ethical frameworks are needed to ensure that companies handle consumer data responsibly, with clear consent and robust protection measures in place. Data breaches and the exploitation of personal information for commercial gain can erode trust in digital platforms, ultimately hindering the growth of digital trade.

Another pressing ethical issue in digital trade is labor rights. As automation and artificial intelligence continue to replace human labor in various sectors, there is concern about the impact on jobs, particularly in low-wage industries. While technological advancements offer increased efficiency and cost savings, they also raise questions about the fairness of the economic benefits that accrue to businesses and consumers. The displacement of workers by machines and AI systems could lead to greater inequality if proper measures are not taken to retrain workers and ensure that they can transition to new roles. Policymakers must address these challenges to create a fair and inclusive digital economy that benefits everyone, not just large corporations.

Additionally, the digital divide remains a significant ethical concern in global trade. While some regions and populations benefit from access to advanced digital technologies, others are left behind due to limited infrastructure, lack of education, and other barriers. This disparity can exacerbate global inequality, as businesses in more developed areas are able to capitalize on digital trade opportunities, while those in underdeveloped regions struggle to participate. Addressing the ethical implications of digital trade requires a commitment to ensuring that technological advancements are accessible to all, fostering a more equitable and sustainable global economy.

13

Opportunities and Challenges Ahead

Chapter 12:

Looking ahead, the future of global trade in the digital age presents both immense opportunities and significant challenges. Emerging technologies such as artificial intelligence, blockchain, and the Internet of Things (IoT) have the potential to transform industries by enabling greater efficiency, transparency, and innovation. Businesses that embrace these technologies can create more agile and competitive supply chains, enhance customer experiences, and reduce operational costs. Furthermore, digital platforms allow for a broader reach, enabling small and medium-sized enterprises to compete on a global scale. This democratization of trade offers exciting prospects for entrepreneurs and businesses worldwide.

However, the path forward is not without its obstacles. One of the biggest challenges is the regulation of digital trade, as existing laws and frameworks struggle to keep pace with rapidly evolving technologies. Issues such as cross-border data flows, cybersecurity, and intellectual property protection are becoming more complex as trade becomes increasingly digital. Governments and international organizations must work together to create a cohesive regulatory environment that balances innovation with security and fairness. Moreover, businesses must adapt to these changing regulatory landscapes to avoid legal pitfalls and maintain consumer trust.

Finally, the future of global digital trade will depend on how well nations can address issues of digital inclusion and equity. As the digital economy grows, it is crucial that all regions and communities are able to participate fully in the global marketplace. Ensuring access to technology, education, and financial services is key to unlocking the potential of digital trade for everyone. If left unaddressed, the digital divide could deepen existing inequalities and limit the benefits of digital trade to a select few. Therefore, fostering a more inclusive digital economy is essential for ensuring that the opportunities of the future are available to all.

14

Conclusion

In conclusion, *Digital Dollars and Global Borders* highlights how technology has revolutionized the way global trade functions. The digital era has drastically altered how businesses and individuals engage in commerce, breaking down geographical boundaries and creating new avenues for economic growth. As the digital landscape continues to evolve, understanding the relationship between digital advancements and international trade becomes essential for anyone seeking to thrive in this interconnected world. The book explores the numerous ways in which digital innovation has reshaped the traditional systems of commerce, offering insights into the future of global markets.

As we continue to embrace these changes, it is crucial to acknowledge both the opportunities and challenges that come with the digital economy. The rapid advancement of digital currencies, e-commerce, and digital services presents unparalleled opportunities for growth, but it also requires navigating complex issues like security, regulation, and ethics. This book emphasizes the need to adapt to these technological shifts thoughtfully and strategically, ensuring that individuals, businesses, and nations are well-prepared to take full advantage of the digital future. By embracing these innovations, we can unlock new economic possibilities and redefine the very nature of trade on a global scale.

Ultimately, *Digital Dollars and Global Borders* serves as both a guide and a call to action for readers to embrace the digital revolution with responsibility and foresight. The future of global trade will be shaped by those who can harness the potential of technology while safeguarding against its risks. This book encourages us to be proactive in shaping an inclusive and sustainable digital economy, one where innovation thrives, and global cooperation transcends borders. Through mindful action, we can ensure that the digital transformation serves the greater good of humanity, opening doors to a more interconnected and prosperous world.

www.ingramcontent.com/pod-product-compliance
Ingram Content Group UK Ltd.
Pitfield, Milton Keynes, MK11 3LW, UK
UKHW020717060225
454761UK00012B/563